PSALM 23 FOR THE SOUL

THE HEALING RENDITION OF PSALM 23 FOR PEOPLE FIGHTING CANCER

MINISTER MERLAND A. BAKER

MINISTER MERLAND A. BAKER

Send written request to:
Merland Baker
P.O. Box 441621
Jacksonville, FL 32244

Printed in the United States of America
ISBN 978-0-9763121-4-7

Disclaimer:
Although the author and publisher have made every effort to ensure that the information in this book was correct at press time, the author and publisher do not assume and hereby disclaim any liability to any party for any loss, damage, or disruption caused by errors or omissions, whether such errors or omissions result from negligence, accident, or any other cause.

This book is not intended as a substitute for the medical advice of physicians. The reader should regularly consult a physician in matters relating to his/her health and particularly with respect to any symptoms that may require diagnosis or medical attention.

DEDICATION

I dedicate this book to my Uncle Ronnie Jones who passed away of brain cancer…Love You Uncle Ronnie.

CONTENT

1   Why This Book…   6

2   What Is Healing?   9

3   Psalm 23 For People Fighting Cancer   12

4   The Daily Declaration Of Healing   14

5   The Healing Hands Of Psalm 23   16

6   ABC'S Of Healing And Encouragement   18

7   Top Ten Healing Psalms   20

8   Determination   24

9   Stories That Inspire Healing   26

10   Seven Days   40

11   You Must Step Before You See It   42

12   How To Keep Your Blessings…   44

13   God As We Know Him   46

LEFT BLANK INTENTIONALLY

ABOUT THE AUTHOR

Minster/Eulogist-Merland has spoken at funerals for deceased friends, family members, loved ones, as well as by request. As a eulogist, Merland delivers personalized messages of hope to console and uplift the hurting and broken hearted.

Writer-Merland has written personalized Psalms, poems, and words of encouragement for those that are dearly departed, lost their jobs, or are simply going through a tough time. His writing style brings comfort and hope to all that read his literature.

Merland is listed on the speaker's bureau of the Florida Association of Christian Schools and Colleges. He holds a bachelor's degree in Sociology and a master's degree in Psychological Studies. He is also a licensed minister and frequently speaks at churches, conferences and school chapels.

Contact Merland at psalm23forthesoul@yahoo.com or merlandbaker@yahoo.com

LEFT BLANK INTENTIONALLY

CHAPTER 1
HOW TO READ THIS BOOK...

You may be wondering why someone would write a chapter about how to read a book.

Do you remember having to memorize a speech, times tables, etc.?

To memorize them you had to practice them over and over again.

This devotional guide was written to help you <u>practice healing</u> *over and over again.*

<u>It is my prayer that the words sink down into your subconscious, producing the outcomes you seek.</u>

In other words, you should meditate upon what you read. What you meditate on can produce miracles. Miracles are a manifestation of mindset (more on that next chapter.)

The chapters are short. In turn, this will help you read through them quickly, building your self-confidence.

The more confident you are. The better you feel about yourself. When you feel better about yourself, healing can work in and through you more effectively.

The Miracle Worker

There is only one miracle worker who has all power in His hands and that is God (Psalm 24:1).

I do not claim to have the power to heal anyone.

However, I know that all things are possible if I believe (Matthew 19:26).

Therefore, I chose to believe that God will use this devotional guide as an instrument of His grace to help individuals like yourself who are <u>seeking healing</u> (Isaiah 55:6).

Healing can really be summed up into one name…Jesus (John 14:6).

He is the perfect example of how God helped people then and how God wants to help you now (Hebrews 13:8).

Let me share a new concept in regards to healing.

This may help you to advance at a **faster** pace in terms of your results.

CHAPTER 2
WHAT IS HEALING?

This may sound like a crazy question. But I am asking it for a reason. Like success, healing is relative.

Let's say someone has back pain to the point where they can only stand for 10 minutes.

Being able to stand for an hour without pain may be healing for them.

The man who could only walk 10 steps without getting tired may feel healed being able to walk for 45 minutes.

Now let me give you my definition of healing...

Healing is a cognitive process that leads to action and promotes physiological and psychological manifestations.

All healing starts in the mind; you have to think you are healed before you can be healed.

Mental cognition (thinking) is a capability (ability).

Capabilities can be improved. Improved capabilities promote the manifestation of healing.

Proof

In Matthew chapter 9 there is a story of a woman who needed healing. She spent 12 years with menstrual bleeding. She had no money because it was spent trying to cure her aliment.

Somehow she heard about Jesus and the miracles of healing He'd performed.

This started her ***cognitive process***. This is evident by Matthew 9:21, *"For she said within herself, If I may but touch his garment, I shall be whole."*

Many bible scholars believe she kept saying that to herself, *"If I may but touch his garment I shall be made whole."*

As a result, it **led to action and she was healed physiologically and (I believe) psychologically**.

Evidenced by what Jesus told her in Matthew 9:22 "Your faith has healed you."

If it happened for her, it can happen for you!

CHAPTER 3
PSALM 23 FOR PEOPLE FIGHTING CANCER

The Lord is my Shepherd
I know you are looking for answers
His love will never fail
As you get treatment for cancer

He has prepared the doctors
And will provide the best medical care
The healing of the Lord
Will always be there

Yea thou you go through chemotherapy
That can feel like the shadow of death
His power is present with you
To restore your soul and health

Surely His goodness and mercy

Will always lead you there
His blessings will never fall short
He won't put more on you than you can bear

Your head is anointed with oil
Your cup overflows indeed
He can heal all types of cancer
God will supply your every need

CHAPTER 4
THE DAILY DECLARATION OF HEALING

Death and life
Is in the power of my tongue
I will speak words, that edify, build up, motivate,
encourage, and bring me closer
To my healing

I speak life
Over my body, over my mind, over my health, over
my money, over my family
Over my situations

I speak death
To destructive behavior, disease, lack, poverty,
sickness, and low self-esteem

I believe
That healing is possible

I believe, that if I stay faithful and connected to God,
I will have the health that I say

My words
Shape my world
And nobody can stop my healing

I forgive myself
And forgive others

I am healed, I am pain free, I am whole, God is
working on me

I am
An original masterpiece, created in the image of God

I speak this
And I believe it...AMEN

CHAPTER 5
THE HEALING HANDS OF PSALM 23

The Lord is my Shepherd
His healing hand let me stay
I endured a rough night
Sickness tried to take me away

Your power and Your Might
Looked illness in the eye
In the midst of the shadow of death
You said I would live and not die

Thy rod and thy staff
Your healing will remain
I now rest beside the still waters
As I praise and proclaim Your name

You prepared a table before me

Sickness was the enemy
But you had other plans
Because You touched me
With Your healing hands

CHAPTER 6
ABC'S OF HEALING AND ENCOURAGMENT

A-Accept that you are being healed now

B-Be grateful that you are still alive

C-Call on Jesus. He is always listening

D-Determine to get better

E-Every day is a blessing to be alive

F-Faith without works is dead

G-Grace and peace will be multiplied to you

H-Healing is your right as a Child of God

I-In everything give him thanks

J-Jesus is the way, the truth, and the life

K-Keep God first in all you do

L-Let no negative words proceed from your mouth

M-Many are the afflictions of the righteous but God delivers them from all

N-Now unto Him who is able to do exceedingly, abundantly above all you ask or think

O-Oh taste and see that the Lord is good

P-Pray without ceasing

Q-Quiet the urge to quit

R-Resist temptation and it will flee from you

S-Say to yourself, "I am getting better day by day, hour by hour, and minute by minute."

T-The race is not given to the strong, neither bread to the wise but to those who endure till the end

U-Use the Bible as a weapon against your illness

V-Verily, Verily, I say unto you, whatsoever ye shall ask the Father in Jesus name, he will give it you.

W-We know that all things are working together for good...

Y-Your healing is here! Believe it and receive it.

Z-Zero in on what you desire from God.

CHAPTER 7
TOP TEN HEALING PSALMS

Psalms 30:2

"I prayed to you, LORD God,
and you healed me..."

Psalms 34:19-20

The LORD's people
may suffer a lot,
but he will always
bring them safely through.
Not one of their bones
will ever be broken.

Psalms 41:1-3

You, LORD God, bless everyone
who cares for the poor,

and you rescue those people
in times of trouble.
You protect them
and keep them alive.
You make them happy here
in this land,
and you don't hand them over
to their enemies.

You always heals them
and restore their strength
when they are sick.

Psalms 43:5

Why am I discouraged?
Why am I restless?
I trust you!
And I will praise you again

because you help me,
and you are my God.

Psalm 91:9-10

The LORD Most High
is your fortress.

Run to him for safety,
and no terrible disasters

will strike you
or your home.

Psalm 103:1-5

With all my heart
I praise the LORD,
and with all that I am
I praise his holy name!

With all my heart
I praise the LORD!
I will never forget
how kind he has been.

The LORD forgives our sins,
heals us when we are sick,
and protects us from death.
His kindness and love
are a crown on our heads.

Each day that we live,
he provides for our needs
and gives us the strength
of a young eagle.

Psalm 27:13-14

but I know I will live
to see how kind you are.
Trust the LORD!
Be brave and strong
and trust the LORD.

Psalm 107:19-20

You were in serious trouble,
but you prayed to the LORD,
and he rescued you.

By the power of his own word,
he healed you
and saved you
from destruction.

Psalm 118:17

And so my life is safe,
and I will live to tell
what the LORD has done.

Proverbs 17:22

A merry heart does good, *like* medicine,
But a broken spirit dries the bones.

CHAPTER 8
DETERMINATION

"DETERMINATION IS THE DIFFERENCE
BETWEEN LIVING YOUR DREAMS VS.
LIVING IN DREADFULNESS" ...*Tony Baker*

Stay determined

Stay bold and you will always make it

Nothing or no one can stop you

Stay the course and you'll go through

Failure is not failure. It is only a state of mind

Outcomes and results are the only things that last

Just look how far you've come

You have gone through worse situations in the past

Shake off all of your challenges

Move the doubt aside

Maintain strong determination and walk with pride

Trouble doesn't last long

Your strength will outlast

Soon and very soon,

This too shall pass...

CHAPTER 9
STORIES THAT INSPIRE HEALING

<u>Fever To Freedom</u>

Matthew 8:14-15

Jesus went to the home of Peter, where he found that Peter's mother-in-law was sick in bed with fever.

He took her by the hand, and the fever left her. Then she got up and served Jesus a meal.

One Touch

Matthew 9:20-22

"A woman who had been bleeding for twelve years came up behind Jesus and barely touched his clothes. She had said to herself, 'If I can just touch his clothes, I will get well.' Jesus turned. He saw the woman and said, 'Don't worry! You are now well because of your faith.' At that moment, she was healed."

Curing Every Disease

Matthew 9:35

"Jesus went to every town and village. He taught in their meeting places and preached the good news about God's kingdom. Jesus also healed every kind of disease and sickness."

<u>10 Lepers Are Healed</u>

Luke 17:12-16

"As he was going into a village, ten men with leprosy came toward him. They stood at a distance and shouted, 'Jesus, Master, have pity on us!' Jesus looked at them and said, 'Go show yourselves to the priests.' On their way, they were healed. When one of them discovered he was healed, he came back, shouting praises to God. He bowed down at the feet of Jesus and thanked him."

<u>Blind Man at Siloam Pool</u>

John 9:6-7

"After Jesus said this, he spit on the ground. He made some mud and smeared it on the man's eyes. Then he said, 'Go and wash off the mud in Siloam Pool.' The man went and washed in Siloam, which means 'One Who Is Sent.' When he had washed off the mud, he could see."

Jesus Heals a Crippled Man
Mark 2:1-12

Jesus went back to Capernaum, and a few days later people heard that he was at home.

Then so many of them came to the house that there wasn't even standing room left in front of the door.

Jesus was still teaching when four people came up, carrying a crippled man on a mat.

But because of the crowd, they could not get him to Jesus. So they made a hole in the roof above him and let the man down in front of everyone.

When Jesus saw how much faith they had, he said to the crippled man, "My friend, your sins are forgiven."

Some of the teachers of the Law of Moses were sitting there. They started wondering,

31

"Why would he say such a thing? He must think he is God! Only God can forgive sins."

Right away, Jesus knew what they were thinking, and he said, "Why are you thinking such things?

Is it easier for me to tell this crippled man that his sins are forgiven or to tell him to get up and pick up his mat and go on home?

I will show you that the Son of Man has the right to forgive sins here on earth." So Jesus said to the man,

"Get up! Pick up your mat and go on home."

The man got right up. He picked up his mat and went out while everyone watched in amazement. They praised God and said, "We have never seen anything like this!"

A Widow's Son
Luke 7:11-17

Soon Jesus and his disciples were on their way to the town of Nain, and a big crowd was going along with them.

As they came near the gate of the town, they saw people carrying out the body of a widow's only son. Many people from the town were walking along with her.

When the Lord saw the woman, he felt sorry for her and said, "Don't cry!"

Jesus went over and touched the stretcher on which the people were carrying the dead boy. They stopped, and Jesus said, "Young man, get up!"

The boy sat up and began to speak. Jesus then gave him back to his mother.

Everyone was frightened and praised God. They said, "A great prophet is here with us! God has come to his people."

News about Jesus spread all over Judea and everywhere else in that part of the country.

Everyone Is Healed

Mark 6:53-56

Jesus and his disciples crossed the lake and brought the boat to shore near the town of Gennesaret.

As soon as they got out of the boat, the people recognized Jesus.

So they ran all over that part of the country to bring their sick people to him on mats. They brought them each time they heard where he was.

In every village or farm or marketplace where Jesus went, the people brought their sick to him. They begged him to let them just touch his clothes, and everyone who did was healed.

No More Swelling

Luke 14:1-6

One Sabbath, Jesus was having dinner in the home of an important Pharisee, and everyone was carefully watching Jesus.

All of a sudden a man with swollen legs stood up in front of him.

Jesus turned and asked the Pharisees and the teachers of the Law of Moses, "Is it right to heal on the Sabbath?"

But they did not say a word.

Jesus took hold of the man. Then he healed him and sent him away.

Afterwards, Jesus asked the people, "If your son or ox falls into a well, wouldn't you pull him out right away, even on the Sabbath?"

There was nothing they could say.

Jesus Heals a Man Who Was Deaf and Could Hardly Talk
Mark 7: 31-37

Jesus left the region around Tyre and went by way of Sidon toward Lake Galilee. He went through the land near the ten cities known as Decapolis.

Some people brought to him a man who was deaf and could hardly talk. They begged Jesus just to touch him.

After Jesus had taken him aside from the crowd, he stuck his fingers in the man's ears. Then he spit and put it on the man's tongue.

Jesus looked up toward heaven, and with a groan he said, "Effatha!"which means "Open up!"

At once the man could hear, and he had no more trouble talking clearly.

Jesus told the people not to say anything about what he had done. But the more he told them, the more they talked about it.

They were completely amazed and said, "Everything he does is good! He even heals people who cannot hear or talk."

CHAPTER 10
SEVEN DAYS

"IT NEVER MATTERS HOW MANY PEOPLE
ARE FOR OR AGAINST YOU. YOU PLUS GOD
ARE ALWAYS THE MAJORITY"... *Tony Baker*

What do you call an 86-year-old woman with the energy of a 20-year-old? The spirit and zest for the life of a teenager.

She has the heart of a worshipper, the class of a first lady, and to top it all off she wears stilettos every day-we call her Mary Barker.

Mary Barker is the hero of many people in her town, and was certainly at my old church.

Recently, she had some health problems. The doctors told her that she had a form of stomach cancer.

She laid in that hospital bed for a couple weeks. The doctors told her that they had to operate to remove her cancer. In typical Ma'Barker fashion she refused the procedure.

As a matter of fact, the last thing she would ever do was take a bunch of medication, let alone allow doctors to perform a major surgery on her.

They gave her 7 days to live. Tears flooded the eyes of many people as the news spread. Seven days is what the doctors said. Well, the doctors did not know Ma' Barker, her faith, or the God she served.

I am glad to report that she out lived the doctor's predictions. Since then, she has gone on to be with her Maker.

However, the morale of the story is this. Doctors may know science, but it is best that you know your God. If you don't, you may very well take your last breath in 7 days, or your seventh day could become the string of many more pleasant times.

Chapter 11
You Must Step Before You See It

IF GOD HAS GIVEN YOU THE VISION TO
SEE IT, HE WILL ALSO GIVE YOU THE
POWER TO POSSESS IT"...*Tony Baker*

For the most part, in order to get paid on a job you must work. Very few companies will pay individuals for work they have not done. The same applies here. No effort, no results.

Have you noticed that God rarely reveals everything there is to know about a new opportunity, dream, destiny or how and when healing takes place?

Maybe this happens because if you knew how things would turn out, there would be no need for faith.

Faith is most needed when you are unsure of yourself and the direction you are headed. When action is required and you are unclear about the effectiveness of the direction you must take, just remember the story of Joshua.

God told Joshua to cross over the Jordan River. But there was no clearance in the waters for him and God's people to cross over. At that point a decision had to be made.

Perhaps it is the same decision that you are contemplating, "Do I follow my faith or do I stay in safety?"

I am sure Joshua was nervous and may have felt unsure about his potential outcome. But when the priest stepped into the water, it gave way to them and they crossed over (Joshua 3:14-16).

Your healing is the same way. When you make up your mind to step into all that God has for you, the things you thought would hinder your progress will start to give way just like the waters did for Joshua and God's Chosen People.

The health, healing, and wholeness, are well within your grasp. However, I must warn you. If you are waiting on your circumstances to be perfect, then you may very well miss crossing over.

Joshua and God's Chosen People were not perfect, but God's ability to make things happen for them was. So stop worrying and start stepping!

Chapter 12
How To Keep Your Blessings

"MAY HE GIVE YOU THE DESIRE OF YOUR
HEART AND MAKE ALL YOUR PLANS
SUCCEED"...*Psalm 20:4 NIV*

Moses is one of the most celebrated leaders of all time. It is often expressed that his biggest problem was his incapability of speaking.

On the contrary, Moses' greatest challenge was not his inability to communicate but his self-limiting belief. Outside of speaking, God showed him several strengths he possessed as well as introduced him to a new level of personal power.

He was shown how a stick can become a snake and how he could alter the pigmentation of his skin. He was even given power over the natural resource of water through his staff.

In spite of God's confirmation and encouragement, Moses still refused to believe in himself. I feel that most people are like Moses. They have tremendous talent but they are tainted with a bottom line self-belief.

It was Moses' lack of self-confidence that grieved God. God wanted to bless Moses in a greater dimension. He wanted to empower him to communicate his message to free the Children of Israel from one of the most powerful men on earth; The Pharaoh of Egypt.

Instead of allowing his blessings to flow, he forfeited them due to fear. God eventually chose Moses' brother Aaron as the spokesman.

Remember, as you seek healing for your health challenge. Keep the faith! Because excuses grieve God. He wants your healing and blessings to flow.

Keep Trusting God!

Chapter 13
GOD AS WE KNOW HIM

"MORE THAN 9 IN 10 (OR 92% OF)
AMERICANS STILL SAY "YES" WHEN ASKED
THE BASIC QUESTION "DO YOU BELIEVE IN
GOD?"-*Gallup Poll*

Perhaps you are in the minority and do not believe in God. Surprisingly, the majority of Americans believe otherwise.

This means that you should consider a higher power. My higher power is Jesus Christ of the Bible.

However, this section is not about you accepting my belief system, but more about you establishing one.

In my opinion a personal faith is very important. I know you may believe in your mother, grandmother, or other relatives and friends.

Throughout the years I have learned that people will fail you. Some of the most important people in my life have failed me. As much as I love my wife, I must admit that she has failed me and likewise I have failed her.

The truth of the matter is this. Your faith in God gives you support from a person that knows more about you than you do about yourself. God as you know Him has a great plan for your life. He desires to fellowship with you through rough times.

God also desires to encourage you when you feel like a failure. He longs to be your friend when others have forsaken you. He has the power to heal any cancer.

In conclusion, I would encourage you to direct or redirect your effort to get a relationship with God.

Think of it this way, if you believe in God then what do you have to lose? You have not lost any money, sleep, or clothing. The truth of the matter is that you will only benefit if you trust God. Furthermore, if you don't believe in God, He believes in you.

If this book helped you please share your story or testimony at: psalm23forthesoul@yahoo.com

Have a little faith!

www.ingramcontent.com/pod-product-compliance
Lightning Source LLC
Chambersburg PA
CBHW060628030426
42337CB00018B/3257